BISHOP'S UNIVERSITY
LIBRARY
LENNOXVILLE

A Garland Series

The English Stage

Attack and Defense 1577 - 1730

A collection of 90 important works
reprinted in photo-facsimile in 50 volumes

edited by

Arthur Freeman

Boston University

Amendments of Mr. Collier's False and Imperfect Citations

by

William Congreve

with a preface
for the Garland Edition by

Arthur Freeman

Garland Publishing, Inc., New York & London

1972

Library of Congress Cataloging in Publication Data

Congreve, William, 1670-1729.
Amendments of Mr. Collier's false and imperfect citations.

(The English stage: attack and defense, 1577-1730)
Reprint of the 1698 ed.
"Wing C5844."
1. Collier, Jeremy, 1650-1726. A short view of the immorality and profaneness of the English stage.
I. Title. II. Series.
PN2047.C62C62 1972 792'.013 73-170439
ISBN 0-8240-0606-2

Printed in the United States of America

Preface

William Congreve replied to Collier's Short View *with some alacrity, his* Amendments of Mr. Collier's False and Imperfect Citations *being advertised 9-12 July in* The Post Man, *less than three months after Collier's assault upon himself. Compared with Sir John Vanbrugh's retaliation this seems far the more coherent and witty in terms of its own time, although Krutch (*Conscience and Comedy *[1949], p. 124) calls it "hastily written and not very successful." It is true that Congreve dwells on Collier's critical exaggeration and verbal inaccuracy for the most part, rather than striking at the root of the quarrel, the alleged praise of vice and ridicule of virtue in his plays and in Vanbrugh's – which Vanbrugh, rather dispiritedly, had attempted with his* Short Vindication *a month before. Perhaps Congreve considered that part of the reply accomplished.*

T. J. Wise identified two issues of Amendments, *the earlier with its half-title blank on the verso, two errata on the verso of the title, and D6 in an* *uncanceled state (Ashley IX, 63; cf. Ashley I, 229). Subsequently there appeared an "Advertisement" on the verso of the half-title, correcting "superstition" to "supposition" on p. 43 (D6^r), and an additional erratum was added to the verso of the title, at which time some trivial alterations were made on the title page itself. Copies with the new π^2 also have a cancel D6, not only altering "superstition" as called for, but deleting an entire paragraph. We have reprinted a copy of the original or uncastrated issue in the possession of the Publishers, and have added as an appendix $\pi 1^v$, $\pi 2^{r\text{-}v}$ and D6$^{r\text{-}v}$, from the Ashley second (corrected) issue, British Museum Ashley 451. The collation is π^2 B-H^8 I^4.*

Lowe-Arnott-Robinson 298; Hooker 13; Wing C5844.

July, 1972 A. F.

Ed: Hector 1789

AMENDMENTS

OF

Mr. COLLIER's

False and Imperfect CITATIONS, &c.

AMENDMENTS
OF
Mr. COLLIER's
False and Imperfect CITATIONS, &c.

From the { OLD BATCHELOUR, DOUBLE DEALER, LOVE for LOVE, MOURNING BRIDE.

By the Author of those Plays.

Quem recitas meus est o Fidentine Libellus,
Sed male dum recitas incipit esse tuus.

Mart.

Graviter, & iniquo animo, maledicta tua paterer, si te scirem Judicio magis, quem morbo animi, petulantia ista uti. Sed, quoniam in te neque modum, neque modestiam ullam animadverto, respondebo tibi: uti, si quam maledicendo voluptatem cepisti, eam male-audiendo amittas.

Salust. Decl.

LONDON,
Printed for *J. Tonson* at the *Judge's Head* in *Fleet-street*, near the *Inner-Temple-Gate.* 1698.

ERRATA.

Page 7. line 23. for *worst* read *worse*; p. 105. l. 13. read *Pantomimes*.

AMENDMENTS OF *Mr.* COLLIER's *False and Imperfect CITATIONS*, &c.

I Have been told by ſome, That they ſhould think me very idle, if I threw away any time in taking notice ev'n of ſo much of Mr. *Collier's* late Treatiſe of the Immorality, *&c.* of the *Engliſh* Stage, as related to my ſelf, in reſpect of ſome Plays written by me: For that his malicious and ſtrain'd Interpretations of my Words were ſo groſs and palpable, that any indifferent and unprejudic'd Reader would immediately condemn him upon his own Evidence, and acquit me before I could make my Defence.

On the other hand, I have been tax'd of Lazineſs, and too much Security in neglecting thus long to do my ſelf a neceſſary Right, which might be effected with ſo very little Pains; ſince very little more is requiſite in my Vindication, than to repreſent truly and at length, thoſe Paſſages which Mr. *Collier* has ſhewn imperfectly, and for the moſt part by halves. I would rather be thought Idle than Lazy; and ſo the laſt Advice prevail'd with me.

I have no Intention to examine all the Abſurdities and Falſhoods in Mr. *Collier*'s Book; to uſe the Gentleman's own Metaphor in his Preface, *An Inventory of ſuch a Ware-houſe would be a large Work.* My Detection of his Malice and Ignorance, of his Sophiſtry and vaſt Aſſurance, will lie within a narrow Compaſs, and only bear a Proportion to ſo much of his Book as concerns my ſelf.

Leaſt

Leaſt of all, would I undertake to defend the Corruptions of the Stage; indeed if I were ſo inclin'd, Mr. *Collier* has given me no occaſion; for the greater part of thoſe Examples which he has produc'd, are only Demonſtrations of his own Impurity, they only ſavour of his Utterance, and were ſweet enough till tainted by his Breath.

I will not juſtifie any of my own Errors; I am ſenſible of many; and if Mr. *Collier* has by any Accident ſtumbled on one or two, I will freely give them up to him, *Nullum unquam ingenium placuit ſine venia.* But I hope I have done nothing that can deprive me of the Benefit of my Clergy; and tho' Mr. *Collier* himſelf were the Ordinary, I may hope to be acquitted.

My Intention therefore, is to do little elſe, but to reſtore thoſe Paſſages to their primitive Station, which have ſuffer'd ſo much in being tranſplanted by him: I will remove 'em from his Dunghil, and replant 'em in the Field of Nature; and when I have waſh'd 'em of that Filth which they have contracted in paſſing thro' his very dirty hands, let their own Innocence protect them.

Mr. *Collier*, in the high Vigour of his Obſcenity, firſt commits a Rape upon my Words, and then arraigns 'em of Immodeſty; he has Barbarity enough to accuſe the very Virgins that he has deflowr'd, and to make ſure of their Condemnation, he has himſelf made 'em guilty: But he forgets that while he publiſhes their ſhame he divulges his own.

His Artifice to make Words guilty of Profaneſs, is of the ſame nature; for where the Expreſſion is unblameable in its own clear and genuine Signification, he enters into it himſelf like the evil Spirit; he poſſeſſes the innocent

nocent Phraſe, and makes it bellow forth his own Blaſphemies; ſo *that one would think the Muſe was Legion.* Coll. p. 81.

To reprimand him a little in his own Words, if theſe Paſſages produc'd by Mr. *Collier* are obſcene and profane, *Why were they rak'd in and diſturb'd unleſs it were to conjure up Vice, and revive Impurities? Indeed Mr.* Collier *has a very untoward way with him; his Pen has ſuch a Libertine Stroke, that 'tis a queſtion whether the Practice or the Reproof be the more licentious.* p. 70, 71.

He teaches thoſe Vices he would correct, and writes more like a Pimp than a P---. Since the buſineſs muſt be undertaken, why was not the Thought blanch'd, the Expreſſion made remote, and the ill Features caſt into Shadows? So far from this, which is his own Inſtruction in his own words, is Mr. *Collier's* way of Proceeding, that he has blackned the Thoughts with his own *Smut*; the Expreſſion that was remote, he has brought nearer; and lest by being brought near its native Innocence might be more visible, he has frequently varied it, he has new-molded it, and stamp'd his own Image on it; so that it at length is become Current Deformity, and fit to be paid into the Devil's Exchequer.

I will therefore take the Liberty to exorcise this evil Spirit, and whip him out of my Plays, where-ever I can meet with him. Mr. *Collier* has revers'd the Story which he relates from *Tertullian*; and after his Visitation of
p. 257. the Play-house returns, having left the Devil behind him.

If I do not return his Civilities in calling him Names, it is because I am not very well vers'd in his *Nomenclatures*; therefore for his *Foot pads*, which he calls us in his Preface, and for his *Buffoons* and *Slaves in the Saturnalia*, which he frequently bestows
p. 81, 63, 175. on us in the rest of his Book, I will onely call him Mr. *Collier*, and that I will

will call him as often as I think he ſhall deſerve it.

Before I proceed, for methods ſake, I muſt premiſe ſome few things to the Reader, which if he thinks in his Conſcience are too much to be granted me, I deſire he would proceed no further in his Peruſal of theſe Animadverſions, but return to Mr. *Collier's Short View*, &c.

Firſt, I deſire that I may lay down *Ariſtotle*'s Definition of Comedy; which has been the Compaſs by which all the Comick Poets, ſince his time, have ſteer'd their Courſe. I mean them whom Mr. *Collier* ſo very frequently calls *Comedians*; for the Diſtinction between *Comicus* and *Comœdus*, and *Tragicus* and *Tragœdus* is what he has not met with in the long Progreſs of his Reading.

Comedy (ſays *Ariſtotle*) is an Imitation of the worſt ſort of People. Μίμησις φαυλοτέρων, *imitatio pejorum*. He does not mean the worſe ſort of People in reſpect to their Quality, but in reſpect to their Manners. This is plain, from his telling you immediately after, that he does not mean Κατὰ πάσαν κακίαν, relating to all kinds of Vice: there are Crimes too daring and too horrid for Comedy. But the Vices moſt frequent, and which are the common Practice of the looſer ſort of Livers, are the ſubject Matter of Comedy. He tells us farther, that they muſt be expoſed after a ridiculous manner: For Men are to be laugh'd out of their Vices in Comedy; the Buſineſs of Comedy is to delight, as well as to inſtruct: And as vicious People are made aſham'd of their Follies or Faults, by ſeeing them expos'd in a ridiculous manner, ſo are good People at once both warn'd and diverted at their Expence.

Thus much I thought neceſſary to premiſe, that by ſhewing the Nature and End of Comedy, we may be prepared to expect Characters agreeable to it.

Secondly, Since Comick Poets are oblig'd by the Laws of Comedy, and to the intent that Comedy may answer its true end and purpose abovementioned, to represent vicious and foolish Characters: In Consideration of this, I desire that it may not be imputed to the Perswasion or private Sentiments of the Author, if at any time one of these vicious Characters in any of his Plays shall behave himself foolishly, or immorally in Word or Deed. I hope I am not yet unreasonable; it were very hard that a Painter should be believ'd to resemble all the ugly Faces that he draws.

Thirdly, I must desire the impartial Reader, not to consider any Expression or Passage cited from any Play, as it appears in Mr. *Collier's* Book; nor to pass any Sentence or Censure upon

upon it, out of its proper Scene, or alienated from the Character by which it is ſpoken; for in that place alone, and in his Mouth alone, can it have its proper and true Signification.

I cannot think it reaſonable, becauſe Mr. *Collier* is pleas'd to write one Chapter of *Immodeſty*, and another of *Profaneneſs*, that therefore every Expreſſion traduc'd by him under thoſe Heads, ſhall be condemn'd as obſcene and profane immediately, and without any further Enquiry. Perhaps Mr. *Collier* is acquainted with the *deceptio viſus*, and preſents Objects to the View through a ſtain'd Glaſs; things may appear ſeemingly profane, when in reality they are only ſeen through a profane *Medium*, and the true Colour is diſſembled by the help of a Sophiſtical Varniſh: Therefore, I demand the Privilege of the *habeas Corpus* Act, that the Priſoners ftners may have Liberty to remove, and to appear before a just Judge in an open and an uncounterfeit light.

Fourthly, Because Mr. *Collier* in his Chapter of the Profaneness of the Stage, has founded great part of his Accusation upon the Liberty which Poets take of using some Words in their Plays, which have been sometimes employed by the Translators of the Holy Scriptures: I desire that the following Distinction may be admitted, *viz.* That when Words are apply'd to sacred things, and with a purpose to treat of sacred things; they ought to be understood accordingly: But when they are otherwise apply'd, the Diversity of the Subject gives a Diversity of Signification. And in truth, he might as well except against the common use of the Alphabet in Poetry, because the same Letters are necessary to the spelling of Words which are mention'd in sacred Writ.

Tho'

Tho' I have thought it requiſite, and but reaſonable to premiſe theſe few things, to which, as to ſo many *poſtulata*, I may when occaſion offers, refer my ſelf; yet if the Reader ſhould have any Objection to the Latitude which at firſt ſight they may ſeem to comprehend, I dare venture to aſſure him that it ſhall be remov'd by the Caution which I ſhall uſe, and thoſe Limits by which I ſhall reſtrain my ſelf, when I ſhall judge it proper for me to refer to them.

It may not be impertinent in this place, to remind the Reader of a very common Expedient, which is made uſe of to recommend the Inſtruction of our Plays; which is this. After the Action of the Play is over, and the Delight of the Repreſentation at an end; there is generally Care taken, that the Moral of the whole ſhall be ſumm'd up, and deliver'd to the Audience, in the very laſt and con-

concluding Lines of the Poem. The Intention of this is, that the Delight of the Repreſentation may not ſo ſtrongly poſſeſs the Minds of the Audience, as to make them forget or overſee the Inſtruction: It is the laſt thing ſaid, that it may make the laſt Impreſſion; and it is always comprehended in a few Lines, and put into Rhyme, that it may be eaſy and engaging to the Memory.

Mr. *Collier* divides his Charge againſt the Stage into theſe four heads, Immodeſty, Profaneneſs, Abuſe of the Clergy, and Encouragement of Immorality.

I have yet written but four poor Plays; and this Author, out of his very particular Favour to me, has found the means to accuſe 'em every one of one or more of theſe four Crimes. I will examine each in its turn, by his Citations; and begin with the Plays in the order that they were written.

In

In his Chapter of the Immodesty
of the Stage, he has not made any
Quotation from my Comedies: But
in general, finds fault with the
lightness of some Characters. He
p.10,12. mentions slightly, and I think without any Accusation, *Belinda* in the
Old Batchelor, and *Miss Prue* in *Love*
for Love. *Miss Prue*, he says, is represented *silly to screen her Impudence*,
which *amounts to this Confession, that*
Women when they have their Under-
p. 11. *standings about them, ought to Converse*
otherwise. I grant it; this is in truth
the Moral of the Character. If
Mr. *Collier* would examine still at
this rate, we should agree very well.
Belinda he produces as a Character
p. 12. *under Disorders of Liberty*; this last
is what I do not understand, and
therefore desire to be excused, if I
can make no Answer to it. I only
refer those two Characters to the
Judgment of any impartial Reader,

to

to determine whether they are represented so as to engage any Spectator to imitate the Impudence of one, or the Affectation of the other; and whether they are not both ridiculed rather than recommended.

But he proceeds, *the Double-dealer is particularly remarkable. There are but four Ladies in this Play, and three of the biggest of them are Whores.* p. 12. These are very *big* Words; very much too *big* for the Sense, for to say *three of the biggest*, when there are but four in Number, is stark Nonsense: Whatever the *Matter* may be in this Gentleman's Book, I perceive his *Stile* at least is admirable.

Well, suppose he had said—— and the three Biggest, *&c.* for I am sure he cannot part with *biggest*, he has occasion to use it so often in the rest of his Book. But mark, he gives us an instance of his *big* good Breeding. *A great Complement to Quality,*

lity, to tell them, there is not above a quarter of them honest! This Computation I suppose he makes by the help of political Arithmetick. As thus; the Stage is the Image of the World; by the Men and Women represented there, are signified all the Men and Women in the World; so that if four Women are shewn upon the Stage, and three of them are vicious, it is as much as to say, that three parts in four of the whole Sex are stark naught. He who dares be so hardy as to gain-say this Argument, let him do it; for my part, I love to meddle with my Match. It was a mercy that all the four Women were not naught; for that had been maintaining that there was not one Woman of Quality honest. What has *Virgil* to answer for at this rate, in his *Æneis*? Where, for two of the Fair Sex that do good, *viz. Venus* and the *Sibyll*,

Sybill, (for *Cybelle* and *Andromache* are but Well-wiſhers) he has the following Catalogue, who are always engag'd in Miſchief, *viz.* *Juno*, *Juturna*, *Dido*, her Siſter, her Nurſe, an old Witch, *Alecto* the Fury, all the *Harpies*; to theſe you are reminded of *Helen* the Firſt Incendiary, *Sylvia* is produc'd as a Second, next *Camilla*, then *Amata*, who deſpiſed the Decrees of the Gods; nay, poor *Creuſa* and *Lavinia* are made ſubſervient to unfortunate Events. This is *Boſſus's* Remark, and he ſays that *Virgil* in the Characters of the Sex, has cloſely obſerved the Rule of *Ariſtotle*, who in his Treatiſe of Poetry has ventur'd to affirm, That there are more bad than good Women in the World; and that they do more harm than good.

Traite du poem. Epiq; L. 4. Cap. 2.

In an Epick Poem Ladies of Quality may be uſed as *Ariſtotle* pleaſes;

but

but Comedy was meant to complement, and tickle, and flatter, and all that.

Here I take the first Liberty to refer the Reader to my first Proposition. Mr. *Collier*, who talks with great Intimacy of Ancient and Modern Criticks, and amongst others, makes familiar mention of *Rapin*, has unluckily overseen a particular Remark that is made by that learned Critick, on the Improvement of Modern Comedy by *Moliere*, in his raising his riculous Characters. If he does not know where to find it, I can help him to it.

Vid.Coll. p. 175.

Les anciens Poetes Comiques n'ont que des Valets pour les plaisans de leur Theatre, et les plaisans du Theatre de Moliere, sont les Marquis et les gens de qualité, les autres n'ont Joüé dans la Comedie, que la vie bourgeoise et commun, et Moliere a Joüé tout Paris et la Cour.

Rap. *Reflex. sur la* Poet. 26.

Well,

Well, this may be the *French*, and it may be the *English* Breeding; but Mr. *Collier* assures us—— *This was not the* Roman *Breeding*. They used to complement Vice in Quality, the gentle *Persius* gives us an Instance of it. p. 12.

Vos o Patricius sanguis, quos vivere fas est
Occipiti cæco, posticæ occurrite sannæ.

Sat. 1.

But *Persius* was a Man of Quality, and perhaps might be a little familiar with his Equals. As for *Juvenal*, he kept his distance, and made it as plain as the Sun.

Namq; ibi fortunæ veniam damus. Alea turpis,
Turpe & adulterium mediocribus: hæc eadem illi
Omnia cum faciant, Hilares nitidiq; vocantur.

Sat. 11.

I am finely employed, to furniſh my Adverſary with two ſuch Authorities againſt my ſelf: But reflecting that Mr. *Collier* has no great Eſteem for *Juvenal*, who he ſays, *writes more like a*
p. 71. *Pimp than a Poet.* 'Tis likely that he will return me his Authority, to make the beſt Uſe that I can of it for my ſelf; therefore I will take the Liberty to ſtate a ſhort Queſtion.

Juvenal by the help of an *Irony*, has in theſe three Lines, laſh'd the Vices of great Perſons with more Severity, than he could have done by the means of a direct and point-blank Invective.
p. 12, 173, 175. Mr. *Collier* is in plain terms, for having Complements paſs'd on Perſons of Quality, and neither will allow their Follies nor their Vices to be expos'd. Now the Queſtion that I would ask, is onely, which agrees beſt with the Character of a Pimp, the Satire of *Juvenal*, or the Complaiſance of

Mr.

Mr. *Collier*? In the Conclusion of his Preface he is quite of another Opinion; there *he confesses he has no Ceremony for Debauchery, for to complement Vice, is but one remove from worshipping the Devil*; now that Mr. *Collier* complements Vice is plain. *Ergo*, &c.

This is his own Confession, and so I leave him to lick himself whole with one of his own Absolutions.

When Vice shall be allowed as an Indication of Quality and good Breeding, then it may also pass for a piece of good Breeding to complement Vice in Quality: But till then, I humbly conceive, that to expose and ridicule it, will altogether do as well.

The Double-dealer (he says) *runs* p. 27.
riot upon some occasion or other, and gives Lord Touchwood *a Mixture of Smut and Pedantry to conclude*

 with:

Had Osmin (says he) *parted with* Almeria *civilly, it had been much better, that rant of* Smut *and* Profaneſs *might*
P. 32, 33, *have been ſpared.* What he means by
34. *civilly* I know not, unleſs he means *dully* and *inſenſibly*; neither Civility nor Incivility have any thing to do with Paſſion; where a Scene is wrought to an Exceſs of Tenderneſs and Grief, there is no room for either Rudeneſs or Complaiſance. Mr. *Collier* is pleas'd to condemn the parting of *Oſmin* and *Almeria*, by comparing it with the meeting of *Menelaus* and *Helen*; but I muſt take the Liberty to tell him, that meeting and parting are two things, and eſpecially between two Lovers. Now for the rant of *Smut* and *Profaneſs*.

Oſm. O my Almeria.
What do the damn'd endure but to deſpair,
But knowing Heav'n to know it loſt for ever.

I will

I will not here ſo much as refer my ſelf to my third Propoſition, nor deſire the Reader to trouble himſelf ſo far, as to look on theſe Lines in their proper Scene and Place, tho' moſt of the foregoing Incidents in the Poem were contrived ſo as to prepare the Violence of this Scene; and all the foregoing part of this Scene was laid as a Gradation of Paſſion, to prepare the violence of theſe Expreſſions, the laſt and moſt extream of the whole, in *Oſmin*'s Part.

For once I will let theſe Lines remain as they are ſet by Mr. *Collier*, with his own filthy Foil beneath, hem'd in and ſullied over with his own *Smut*. And ſtill what is there either of Profaneſs or Immodeſty in the Expreſſion? Is not the Reflection rather moral and religious than otherwiſe? Does not the Alluſion ſet forth the terrors of Damnation? I dare affirm that Mr. *Col-*

lier himſelf, cannot ſo tranſpoſe thoſe words as to make 'em ſignifie any thing either *ſmutty* or *profane* : What he may be able to do with the Letters if they were disjointed, I know not ; I will not diſpute his Skill in *Anagram*; and if the truth were known, I believe there lies the Streſs of his Proof. Well, Mr. *Saygrace*, in the *Double-dealer*, is beholding to him for his new Amuſement, for the future he ſhall renounce Acroſticks and purſue *Anagrams*.

As to what he ſays after, that theſe Verſes are a ſimilitude drawn from the Creed ; I no more underſtand it, than he himſelf would believe it, tho' he ſhould affirm it.

In the reſt of his Remarks upon this Scene, his *Zeal* gives way to his *Criticiſm*; he had but an ill hold of *Profaneſs*, and was reduc'd to catch at the *Poetry*. The corruption of a rotten Divine is the Generation of a ſowr Critick.

He

He is very merry, and as he ſuppoſes with me; in laughing at *waſting Air*. *Waſting* he thinks is a ſenſeleſs *Epithet* for *Air*, truly I think ſo too. I will not loſe this occaſion of conſenting with him, becauſe he will not afford me many more: But where does he meet with *waſting Air*? not in the *Mourning-bride*; for in that Play it is printed *wafting Air*, ſo that all his awkard Railery about this word, reflects alone upon himſelf: To ſay nothing of his Honeſty in making a falſe Quotation, or of his becoming aſſurance in charging me with his own Nonſenſe.

He proceeds in his unlucky and ſatirical Strain, and ridicules half a dozen Epithets, and about as many Figures, which follow in the ſame Scene, with much Delicacy of fine Railery, Excellence of good Manners, and Elegancy of Expreſſion.

Almeria,

Almeria, in the Play, oppreſs'd and ſinking beneath her Grief, adapts her words to her Poſture, and ſays to *Oſmin*——

—— O let us not ſupport,
But ſink each other lower yet, down, down,
Where levell'd low, &c.

One would think (ſays Mr. *Collier*) *ſhe was learning a Spaniel to ſet.*

Learning a Spaniel to ſet! *Delectus verborum eſt Origo eloquentiæ*, is an Aphoriſm of *Julius Cæſar*, and Mr. *Collier* makes it plain. This poor Man does not ſo much as underſtand even his own Dog-language, when he ſays *learning*, I ſuppoſe he means *teaching a Spaniel to ſet*, a dainty Critick, indeed!

A little before, *Almeria* is cold, faint and trembling in her Agony, and ſays,

—*I chatter, ſhake and faint with thrilling fears.*

By the way (ſays Mr. *Collier*, for now he is Mr. *Collier emphatically*) *'tis a mighty wonder to hear a Woman chatter! but there is no Jeſting*, &c.

Jeſting quotha! What, does he take the letting a Pun to be the breaking of a Jeſt? a Whip and a Bell, and away with him to Kennel again immediately.

Ay, now he's in his Element, as you ſhall hear.

This litter of Epithets makes the Poem look like a Bitch over-ſtock'd with Puppies, and ſucks the Sence almoſt to skin and bone. The Compariſon is handſome, I muſt needs ſay; but I deſire the Reader to conſider that it is Mr. *Collier* the Critick, that talks at this odd rate; not Mr. *Collier* the Divine: I would not, by any means, that

that he ſhould miſtake one for the other.

If it is neceſſary for me to give any reaſon in this place, why I have uſed Epithets and Figures in this Scene, I will do it in few words. Firſt I deſire the Reader to remove my Verſes from amongſt Mr. *Collier*'s Interlineations of ſad Drollery; and reinſtate 'em in the Scene of the Play from whence they were torn. If there is found Paſſion in thoſe parts of the Scene where thoſe Epithets and Figures are uſed, they will ſtand in need of no Vindication; for every body knows that Diſcourſes of men in Paſſion, naturally abound in Epithets and Figures, in Agravations and Hyperboles. To this I add, That the Diction of Poetry conſiſts of Figures; by the frequent uſe of bold and daring Figures, it is diſtinguiſh'd from Proſe and Oratory. Epithets are beautiful in Poetry, but make Proſe

lan-

languiſhing and cold; and the frequent uſe of them in Proſe, makes it pretend too much and approach too near to Poetry. If Figures and Epithets are natural to Paſſion, and if they compoſe the Diction of Poetry, certainly Tragedy, which is of the ſublime and firſt-rate Poetry, and which ought every where to abound in *Paſſion*, may very well be allow'd to uſe Epithets and Figures, more eſpecially in a Scene conſiſting entirely of Paſſion, and ſtill more particularly in the moſt violent part of that Scene. Thus much, to juſtifie the uſe and frequency of Epithets and Figures in the Scene abovementi-on'd. Ay, but Mr. *Collier* ſays ſome of the Figures there are *Stiff*: He ſays ſo, I confeſs; but what then? Why in anſwer, I ſay they are not, and ſo leave it to be determin'd by better Judges.

Ariſt. Rhet. L. 3. C. 3.

Having

Having ſhewn that men in Paſſion, naturally make uſe of violent Figures and Epithets ; I will produce no leſs a Man than Mr. *Collier* himſelf for an Example : If you would behold the Gentleman beginning to ſwell, ſee him in Page 80. there he puffs and blows, and deals mightily in ſhort periods : At firſt he is ſcarce able to Breath, but at length he O-pens ; and anon finds vent for a very odd Expreſſion. He is angry with ſome Play or other, and ſays-.- *Nature made the ferment and riſing of the Blood, for ſuch occaſions.* I hope he ſpeaks Figuratively, or elſe I am ſure he ſpeaks at leaſt Prophanely ; for we know who is meant by *Nature in the Language of Chriſtianity, and*
v. p. 72. *eſpecially under the Notion of a* Maker.

He diſcovers in this Expreſſion, that his Religion and his Natural Philoſophy are both of a ſize.

He

He has declared the very Source of Living, and the Spring of Motion in the Mechanical Part of Man, to be no more than the Fountain-Head of Follies and Paſſions; and intimates very ſtrongly, That *Nature* made it only for that purpoſe.

But I think nothing that he ſays, ſhould be conſider'd ſeriouſly; therefore I will proceed, and produce Mr. *Collier* as he ſtands advanc'd both in *ferment* and *figure*. In (p. 84.) he has drawn Quotations from Comedies, *that look Reeking as it were from* Pandemonium, *and almoſt ſmell of Fire and Brimſtone; Eruptions of Hell with a witneſs! He almoſt wonders the Smoak of them has not darkned the Sun, and turn'd the Air to Plague and Poiſon. Provocations enough to Arm all Nature in Revenge; to exhauſt the Judgments of Heaven*, &c. He goes on with ſuch terrible Stuff for a conſiderable while together. I give this only as a Sample

 of

of ſome of this Gentleman's Figures.

Methinks I hear him pronounce 'em every time I behold 'em, they are almoſt Noiſy and Turbulent, even in the Print. In ſhort, they are Contagious; and I find he that will ſpeak of them, is in great danger to ſpeak like them. But why does Mr. *Collier* uſe all this Vehemence in a Written Argument? If he were to Preach, I grant it might be neceſſary for him to make a Noiſe, that he might be ſure to be heard: But why all this Paſſion upon Paper? Judgment is never Outrageous; and Chriſtianity is ever Meek and Mild.

I have read it ſomewhere as the Remark of St. *Chryſoſtom*, That the Prophets of God were as much diſtinguiſh'd from the Prophets of the Devil by their Behaviour, as by the Divine Truths which they utter'd. The former gave Oracles with all Mildneſs and Temper; the other were ever

Bellow-

Bellowing with Fury and Madneſs; no wonder (ſays he) for the firſt were inſpir'd with the Holy Ghoſt; and the laſt were poſſeſs'd with the Devil. So the reaſon is plain.

But I have employ'd too much time in digreſſing from my purpoſe, which is chiefly to Vindicate my ſelf; and only from Caſual Obſervation, to take Notice of Mr. *Colliers* Errors, as they ſhall appear Blazing up and down in thoſe Pages where I am concern'd, or others into which I may dip accidentally, in ſearching for Expreſſions cited from my own Plays.

I have done with him in his Chapter of Immodeſty. The Reader has ſeen his Charge againſt the *Mourning Bride*, and is a Judge of the Juſtneſs and Strength of it. I confeſs I have not much to ſay in Commendation of any thing that I have Written: But if a fair-dealing-man, or a candid Critick had examin'd that Tragedy, I fancy that neither the general Moral contain'd in the two laſt Lines; nor the ſeveral particular Morals interwoven with the ſucceſs of every principal Character, would have been overſeen by him.

The Reward of Matrimonial Conſtancy in *Almeria*, of the ſame Virtue, together with filial Piety and Love to his Country in *Oſmin*; the Puniſhment of Tyranny in *Manuel*, of Ambition in *Gonzalez*, of violent Paſſions, and unlawful Love in *Zara*: Theſe it may be were Parts of the Poem as worthy to be obſerved, as one or two erroneous Expreſſions; and admit they were ſuch, might in ſome meaſure have aton'd for them.

Mr. *Collier* in his ſecond Chapter, Charges the Stage with Profaneſs. Almoſt all the Quotations which he has made from my Plays in this Chapter are repreſented falſly, or by halves;

ſo

ſo that I have very little to do in their Vindication, but to repreſent 'em as they are in the Original, fairly and at length; and to fill up the Blanks which this worthy honeſt Gentleman has left.

In the Old Batchelour (ſays he) *Vainlove asks* Bellmour, *Could you be content to go to Heav'n?* Coll. P. 62.

Bell. *Hum, not immediately, in my Conſcience not Heartily* -----

Here Mr. *Collier* concludes this Quotation with a daſh, as if both the Senſe and the Words of the whole Sentence, were at an end. But the remainder of it in the Play *Act.* 3. *Scene* 2. is in theſe words --- *I would do a little more good in my generation firſt, in order to deſerve it.*

I think the meaning of the whole is very different from the meaning of the firſt half of this Expreſſion. 'Tis one thing for a Man to ſay poſitively, he will not go to Heaven; and another to ſay, that he does not think himſelf worthy, till he is better prepared. But Mr. *Collier* undoubtedly was in the right, to take juſt as much as would ſerve his own turn. The Stile of this Expreſſion is Light, and ſuitable to Comedy, and the Character of a wild Debauchee of the Town; but there is a Moral meaning contain'd in it, when it is not repreſented by halves.

From Scene 3. of the 4*th* Act of the ſame Comedy, he makes the following Quotation. *Fondlewife* a Jealous Puritan is obliged for ſome time to be abſent from his Wife:

Fond. *Have you throughly conſider'd how deteſtable, how heinous, and how Crying a Sin the ſin of Adultery is? Have you weigh'd it, I ſay? for it is a very weighty ſin: and although it may lie ---- yet thy Husband muſt alſo bear his part; for thy Iuiquity will fall upon his Head.* Here is another Daſh in this Quotation, I refer the Reader to the Play

to

to ſee what words Mr. *Collier* has Omitted; and from thence he may gueſs at the Strength of his Imagination.

For this Quotation, the Reader ſees it in the ſame Condition that Mr. *Collier* thinks fit to ſhew it: His Notes upon it are as follow.

This fit of Buffoonry and Profaneneſs, was to ſettle the Conſcience of Young Beginners, and to make the Terrors of Religion inſignificant.

Indeed I cannot hold Laughing, when I compare his dreadful Comment with ſuch poor ſilly words as are in the Text: eſpecially when I reflect how *young a beginner*, and how very much a Boy I was when that Comedy was Written; which ſeveral know was ſome years before it was Acted: When I wrote it I had little thoughts of the Stage; but did it to amuſe my ſelf in a ſlow Recovery from a Fit of Sickneſs. Afterwards through my Indiſcretion it was ſeen ; and in ſome little time more it was Acted : And I through the remainder of my Indiſcretion, ſuffer'd my ſelf to be drawn in, to the proſecution of a difficult and thankleſs Study ; and to be involved in a perpetual War with Knaves and Fools. Which reflection makes me return to the Subject in hand.

Bellmour *deſires* Lætitia *to give him leave to Swear by her Eyes and her Lips.* Well, I am very glad Mr. *Collier* has ſo much Devotion for the Lips and Eyes of a Pretty Woman, that he thinks it Profanation to Swear by 'em. I'll give him up this, if he pleaſes. To the next.

He kiſſes the Strumpet, and tells her--- Eternity was in that Moment.

To ſay *Eternity is in a Moment,* is neither Profane nor Sacred, nor good nor bad. With Reverence of my Friend the Author be it ſpoken, I take it to

be

be ſtark Nonſenſe; and I had not cared if Mr. *Collier* had diſcover'd it..

Something or other he ſaw amiſs in it, and Writing a Chapter of Profaneneſs at that time, like little *Bays*, he popt it down for his own.

Lætitia when her Intrigue was like to be diſcover'd, ſays of her Lover,

> *All my Comfort lies in his Impudence, and Heav'n be praiſ'd, he has a conſiderable Portion.*

This Mr. *Collier* calls the *Play-houſe Grace.* It is the expreſſion of a wanton and a vicious Character, in the Diſtreſs and Confuſion of her Guilt. She is diſcover'd in her Lewdneſs, and ſuffer'd to come no more upon the Stage.

In the end of the laſt Act *Sharper* ſays to *Vain-love*:

> *I have been a kind of Godfather to you yonder:*
> *I have promis'd and vow'd ſome things in your name, which I think you are bound to perform.*

I

I meant no ill by this Allegory, nor do I perceive any in it now. Mr. *Collier* ſays it was meant for Drollery on the Catechiſm; but he has a way of diſcovering Drollery where it never was intended; and of intending Drollery where it can never be diſcovered. So much for the *Old Batchelour*.

In the *Double-Dealer* (he ſays) *Lady Plyant cries out Jeſu, and talks Smut in the ſame Sentence.* That Exclamation I give him up freely. I had my ſelf long ſince condemn'd it, and reſolv'd to ſtrike it out in the next Impreſſion. I will not urge the *folly*, viciouſneſs, or affectation of the Character to excuſe it. Here I think my ſelf oblig'd to make my Acknowledgments for a Letter which I receiv'd after the Publication of this Play, relating to this very Paſſage. It came from an Old Gentlewoman and a Widow, as ſhe ſaid, and very well to paſs: It contain'd very good

good Advice, and requir'd an Anſwer, but the Direction for the Superſcription was forgot. If the good Gentlewoman is yet in being, I deſire her to receive my Thanks for her good Counſel, and for her Approbation of all the Comedy, that Word alone excepted.

That Lady *Plyant* talks *Smut* in the ſame Sentence, lies yet upon Mr. *Collier* to prove. His bare Aſſertion without an Inſtance, is not ſufficient. If he can prove that there is downright *Smut* in it, why e'en let him take it for his pains: I am willing to part with it.

His next Objection is, that Sir *Paul*, who he obſerves bears the Character of a Fool, makes mention too often of the word *Providence*; for ſays Mr. *Collier, the meaning muſt be* (by the way, that *muſt* is a little hard upon me) *that Providence is a ridiculous Superſtition; and that none but Blockheads pretend to Religion.* What will it avail me in this place to ſignifie my own meaning, when

P. 62.

when this modeſt Gentleman ſays, I *muſt* mean quite contrary? I am Civiller to him; I take his Senſe as he would have it underſtood; Though his Expreſſion is exquiſite Nonſenſe: and I humbly conceive he may mean, that *a Belief in Providence is a ridiculous Superſtition*, when he ſays that *Providence is a ridiculous Superſtition*,

Lady Froth is pleas'd to call Jehu *a Hackney Coachman.* (ibid.)

Lady *Froth*'s words are as follow-- *Our Jehu was a Hackney Coachman when my Lord took him.* Which is as much as to ſay, that the Coachman's Name is *Jehu*: And why might it not be *Jehu* as well as *Jeremy*, or *Abraham*, or *Joſeph*, or any other Jewiſh or Chriſtian Name? *Brisk* deſires that this may be put into a Marginal Note in Lady Froth's Poem.

This Mr. *Collier* ſays, is meant to *burleſque the Text, and Comment under one.* What Text, or what Comment,

or

or what other earthly Thing he can mean, I cannot poſſibly imagine. Theſe Remarks are very Wiſe ; therefore I ſhall not Fool away any time about them.

Sir *Paul* tells his Wife, *he finds Paſſion coming upon him by Inſpiration.* P. 64.

The poor Man is troubled with the *Flatus*, his Spleen is pufft up with Wind ; and he is likely to grow very angry and peeviſh on the ſuddain ; and deſires the privilege to Scold and give it Vent. The word *Inſpiration* when it has *Divine* prefix'd to it, bears a particular and known ſignification : But otherwiſe, to *inſpire* is no more than to *Breath into* ; and a Man without profaneneſs may truly ſay, that a Trumpet, a Fife, or a Flute, deliver a Muſical Sound, by the help of Inſpiration. I refer the Reader to my fourth Propoſition, in this Caſe. For a Diſpute about this word, would be very like the Con-

troverſie

troverſie in *Ben. Johnſon's* *Barthol. Fair*, between the *Rabbi* and the *Puppet*; it *is* profane, and it *is not* profane, is all the Argument the thing will admit of on either ſide.

*The Double-dealer is not yet exhauſted.*ib.

That is, Mr. *Collier* is not yet exhauſted; for to give double Interpretations to ſingle Expreſſions, with a deſign only to lay hold of the worſt, is double dealing in a great degree.

Cynthia the top Lady grows thoughtful. Cynthia it ſeems is the Top Lady now; not long ſince, the other Three were
P. 12. the three *biggeſt*. Perhaps the Gentleman ſpeaks as to perſonal proportion, *Cynthia* is the Talleſt, and the other Three are the Fatteſt of the Four.

Well. *Cynthia is thoughtful, and upon the queſtion relates her Contemplation.*

Cyn. *I am thinking, that though Marriage makes Man and Wife one Fleſh, it leaves them two Fools.*

Here

Here he has filch'd out a little word so slily, 'tis hardly to be miss'd; and yet without it, the words bear a very different signification. The Sentence in the Play is Printed thus --- *Though Marriage makes Man and Wife one Flesh, it leaves 'em STILL two Fools.* Which by means of that little word *still*, signifies no more, than that if two People were Fools, before or when they were married, they would continue in all probability to be Fools still, and after they were married. *Ben. Johnson* is much bolder in the first Scene of his *Bartholomew Fair.* There he makes Littlewit say to his Wife --- *Man and Wife make one Fool*; and yet I don't think he design'd even that, for a Jest either upon *Genesis* 2. or St. *Matthew* 19. I have said nothing comparable to that, and yet Mr. *Collier* in his penetration has thought fit to accuse me of nothing less.

Thus

Thus I have ſumm'd up his Evidence againſt the *Double-dealer*. I have not thought it worth while to Croſs-examine his Witneſſes very much, becauſe they are generally ſilly enough to detect themſelves.

In *Love* for *Love*, *Scandal* tells
P. 74. Mrs. *Foreſight*, he will *die a Martyr rather than diſclaim his Paſſion*. The word Martyr is here uſed Metaphorically to imply Perſeverance. *Martyr* is a Greek word, and ſignifies in plain Engliſh, no more then a *Witneſs*. A holy Martyr, or a Martyr for Religion is one thing; a wicked Martyr, or Martyr for the Devil is another: A Man may be a Martyr that is a Witneſs to Folly, to Error, or Impiety. *Mr. Collier* is a Martyr to Scandal and Falſhood quite through his Book. This Expreſſion he ſays, is *dignifying Adultery with the Stile of Martyrdom*; as if any word could dignifie Vice.

These

These are very trifling Cavils, and I think all of this kind may reasonably be referr'd to my Fourth Proposition.

> *Jeremy who was bred at the University, calls the natural Inclinations to Eating and Drinking, Whoreson Appetites.* Ibid.

Jeremy bred at the University! Who told him so? What *Jeremy* does he mean, *Jeremy Collier*, or *Jeremy Fetch*? The last does not any where pretend to have been bred there. And if the t'other would but keep his own Counsel, and not Print *M. A.* on the Title Page of his Book, he would be no more suspected of such an Education than his Name-sake. *Jeremy* in the *Play*, banters the Coxcomb *Tattle*, and tells him he has been at *Cambridge*: Whereupon *Tattle* replies ---

> *'Tis well enough for a Servant to be bred at an University.*

Which is ſaid to expoſe the impudence of illiterate Fops, who ſpeak with Contempt of Learning and Univerſities. For the word *Whoreſon*, I had it from *Shakeſpear* and *Johnſon*, who have it very often in their Low Comedies ; and ſometimes their Characters of ſome Rank uſe it. I have put it into the Mouth of a Footman. 'Tis not worth ſpeaking of. But Mr. *Collier* makes a terrible thing of it, and compares it to the *Language of Manicheans, who made the Creation to be the Work of the Devil.* After which he civilly ſolves all by ſaying, *the Poet was* Jeremy's *Tutor, and ſo the Myſtery is at an end.* This by a Periphraſis is calling me *Manichean* ; well let him call me what he pleaſes, he cannot call me *Jeremy Collier.*

His next Quotation is of one line taken out of the middle of eight more in a Speech of Sir *Sampſon* in the ſecond Act of this Comedy : he repre-

ſents

ſents it as an Aphoriſm by it ſelf, and without any regard to what either precedes or follows it. I deſire to be excuſed from tranſcribing the whole Scene or Speech. I refer to my third Propoſition, and deſire the Reader to view it in its place. Mr. *Collier's* Citaon is---*Nature has been provident only to Bears and Spiders.* I beg the Reader to peruſe that Scene, and than to look into the 139 *Pſalm*, becauſe *Mr. Collier* ſays it is paraphraſed by me in this Place. I wonder how ſuch remote Wickedneſs can enter into a Man's Head. I dare affirm the Scene has no more reſemblance of the *Pſalm*, than *Mr. Collier* has of the Character of a Chriſtian Prieſt, which he gives us in page 127, 128. of his own Book. Towards the end of the third Act, *Scandal* has occaſion to flatter Old *Foreſight.* He talks to him, and humours him in the Cant of his own Character, recites Quotations in fa-

vour of Aſtrology, and tells him the wiſeſt Men have been beholding to
p. 75. that Science---

Solomon (ſays he) *was Wiſe, but how? By his Judgment in Aſtrology.* So *ſays* Pineda *in his third Book and eight Chap.* But the Quotation of the Authority is omitted by Mr. *Collier*, either becauſe he would repreſent it as my own Obſervation to ridicule the Wiſdom of *Solomon*, or elſe becauſe he was indeed Ignorant that it belong'd to any Body elſe.

The Words which gave me the Hint are as above cited. *Pin. de rebus Salom.*

> ---*Illum Judiciariam Aſtrologiam calluiſſe circa naturalia, circa inclinationes hominum*, &c.

Do's Mr. *Collier* believe in Prognoſtications from Judicial Aſtrology? Do's he think that *Solomon* had his Wiſdom only from thence? If he does not, why will he not permit the Superſtitions growing from that Science

ence to be expos'd? Why will he not underſtand that the expoſing them in this Place and Manner, does not ridicule the Wiſdom of *Solomon*, but the Folly of *Foreſight*?

Scandal he ſays, continues his Banter, and ſays, *The Wiſe Men of the Eaſt ow'd their Inſtruction to a Star, which is rightly obſerv'd by* Gregory *the Great, in favour of Aſtrology.*

Scandal indeed Banters *Foreſight*, but he does not banter the Audience, in mentioning *Gregory* the Great: Take his own Words.

> *Deus accommodate ad eorum ſcientiam docuit, ut qui in Stellarum Obſervatione verſabantur ex ſtellis Chriſtum diſcerent.*

The reſt of the Banter is what *Scandal* relates from *Albertus Magnus*, who makes it the moſt *valuable Science, becauſe it teaches us to conſider the Cauſation of Cauſes in the Cauſes of things.*

logue of the Play, as if a new Character were introduc'd. A third uſe of this pretended madneſs is, that it gives a Liberty to Satire; and authoriſes a Bluntneſs, which would otherwiſe have been a Breach in the Manners of the Character. Mad-men have generally ſome one Expreſſion which they uſe more frequently than any other. *Valentine* to prepare his Satire, fixes on one which may give us to underſtand, that he will ſpeak nothing but Truth; and ſo before and after moſt of his Obſervations ſays---*I am Truth*. For example. *Foreſight* asks him

----- *What will be done at Court?*

Val. *Scandal will tell you --- I am Truth, I never come there.*

I had at firſt made him ſay, *I am Tom-tell-troth*; but the ſound and meanneſs of the Expreſſion diſpleas'd me: and I alter'd it for one ſhorter, that might ſignifie the ſame thing. What a Charitable and Chriſtian-like Con-

ſtruction

ſtruction my dear Friend *Mr. Collier* has given to this Expreſſion, is fit only to be ſeen in his own Book; and thither I refer the Reader: I will only repeat his Remark as it perſonally aims at me --- *Now a Poet that had not been ſmitten with the pleaſure of Blaſphemy, would not have furniſh'd Frenzy with Inſpiration*, &c. Now I ſay, a Prieſt who was not himſelf furniſh'd with Frenzy inſtead of Inſpiration, would never have miſtaken one for the other.

In his next Chapter he Charges the Stage with the Abuſe of the Clergy. He quotes me ſo little in this Chapter, and has ſo little reaſon even for that little, that it is hardly worth examining.

The *Old Batchelour* has a *Throw* (as he calls is) at the diſſenting Miniſters. P. 101.

Now this *Throw*, in his own Words, amounts to no more than that a Pimp pro-

provides the Habit of a dissenting Minister, as the safest Disguise to co conceal a Whoremaster: Which is rather a Complement than an Affront to the Habit.

Barnaby calls another of that Character Mr. Prig. Calls him Mr. *Prig?* Why what if his Name were Mr. *Prig?* Or what if it were not? This is furiously simple! *Fondlewife to hook in the Church of* England *into the Abuse, tacks a Chaplain to the End of the Description.*

How this pretty little Reasoner has (as he calls it) hook't in the Church of *England?* Can't a Man be a Chaplain unless he is of the Church of *England?*

Father *Dominick* the *2d.* he's for bringing in Heav'n and the Church by hook or crook into his Quarrel. If a *Mufti* had been tack'd to the Description, he would have been equally offended; for *Mufti* in the Language of of the Theater, he ſays, ſignifies *Biſhop*. P. 103.

Maskwell in the *Double Dealer*, has a Plot, and is for engaging *Saygrace* in it. He is for *inſtructing the Levite*, and ſays, *without one of them have a Finger in't, no Plot, publick or private, can expect to proſper*. P. 102.

Perhaps that is a Miſtake; many damnable Plots have miſcarried, wherein Prieſts have been concern'd.

After this, he has tranſcrib'd a broken Piece of a Dialogue between *Maskwell* and *Saygrace*, which I leave to ſhift for it ſelf; having nothing in it worth an Accuſation, or needing a Defence.

Mr. *Collier* is very florid in this Chapter; but it is very hard to know what he would be at. He ſeems to be be apprehenſive of being brought upon the Stage, and in ſome Places endeavours to prove, that as he is a Prieſt, he ſhould be exempted from the Correction of the *Drama*. P. 124, 127.

In

In other Places he does not seem to be averse to treading the Stage; but he would do it in Buskins: He would be *all Gold, Purple, Scarlet, and Embroidery; and as rich as Nature, Art, and*
p. 118. *Rhetorick, can make him.*

We will first enquire whether he may be brought on the Stage or not; and then shew both how he would, and how he should be represented; granting the Representation of his Character to be lawful.

p. 127. Here he lays down something with the appearing face of an Argument, under 3. Heads, to shew that the Clergy have a *Right to Regard and fair Usage*. I'm sure I will never dispute that with him in the general Terms. But I suppose he is particular here; and means that they have a Right to be exempted from the Theater. Whether they have or not I will not pretend to determin; This I know, that the Custom of the Theater in all Ages and Countries is against this

this Opinion ; which in this Chapter is ſufficiently prov'd by the Examples which himſelf has produc'd.

If Mr. *Collier* is in earneſt of that Opinion, he has behav'd himſelf either very treacherouſly or very weakly, in offering to aſſert it by a falſe and a ſophiſtical Argument. His Proof begins. 1.Becauſe of their relation to theDeity.

Now(ſays he) the Credit of the Service always riſes in Proportion to the Quality and Greatneſs of the Maſter. Upon this Poſition he builds all the argument under this firſt Head. The Poſition is ſophiſtical,& hisInferences conſequently falſe.The trick lies here. It being granted him that the Credit of the *Service* riſes in Proportion, *&c.* he ſlily infers, that the Credit of the *Servant* alſo riſes in proportion to the Credit of the *Service*,which is falſe: For every body knows that an ill Servant both diſcredits his Service, and is diſcredited by it. And by how much the more honourable

ble the Service is in which he is employ'd, ſo much the more is he accounted an ill Man who behaves himſelf unworthily in that Service.

If an offending Servant is puniſh'd by the Law, the honour of the Service is not by that means violated; ſo far from that, that it is rather vindicated: Neither on the Stage is the divine Service ridicul'd, only the ridiculous Servant is expos'd.

2. Becauſe of the Importance of their Office. And,

3. They have Preſcription for their Privilege, their Function has been in Poſſeſſion of Eſteem in all Ages and Countries.

Theſe 2. are but Branches of the firſt Head: for *their relation to the Deity* implies the *importance of their Office*; and beſpeaks that Privilege and Eſteem which ever ought to be paid to their Holy Function.

But here again Mr. *Collier* confounds the

the Function with the Person, the Service with the Servant: He is Father *Dominick* still.

I would ask Mr. *Collier* whether a Man, after he has receiv'd holy Orders, is become incapable of either playing the Knave, or the Fool?

If he is not incapable, it is possible that some time or other his Capacity may exert it self to Action.

If he is found to play the Knave, he is subject to the Penalties of the Law, equally with a Lay-man; if he plays the Fool, he is equally with a Lay-fool, the subject of Laughter and Contempt.

By this Behaviour the *Man* becomes alienated from the *Priest*; as such Actions are in their own nature separate and very far remov'd from his function, and when such a one is brought on the Stage, the folly is expos'd, not the function; the *Man* is ridicul'd, and not the *Priest*.

Such a Character neither does nor can asperse the sacred Order of Priesthood,

hood, neither does it at all reflect upon the persons of the pious and good Clergy: For as *Ben. Johnson* observes on the same occasion from St. *Hierome*, *Ubi generalis est de vitiis disputatio, Ibi nullius esse personæ injuriam*, where the business is to expose and reprehend Folly and Vice in general, no particular person ought to take offence. And such business is properly the business of Comedy.

That this may not look like a sophistical distinction in me, to say that the *Man* does, by his behaviour, as it were alienate himself from the *Priest*, and become liable to an ill Character, apart from his Office: I desire it may be observ'd that the Church it self makes the same Distinction.

It was foreseen by the Reverend Bishops and Clergy of this Realm, in their Convocations for establishing the 39. Articles of our Religion in the Years 1562. and 1604. that evil Men (unperceiv'd to be such) might

creep

creep into the Miniſtry of the Church. That afterwards they might become openly profligate, and notoriouſly Scandalous in their Lives and Converſations; even to that Degree, that ſome ſcrupulous Chriſtians, and of a very tender Conſcience, might probably take ſuch Offence at the unworthineſs of their Miniſter, as dangerouſly to avoid his Adminiſtration of the Holy Word and Sacraments: To refrain from publick Worſhip, and to loſe the real Benefit of the Communion, thro' a miſconceiv'd Opinion of the invalidity of it when Adminiſtred by unclean and wicked Hands.

They might (and not without ſome reaſonable Grounds) doubt whether the ſame Man who was perſonally Impious, could be ſpiritually Sacred; whether he who by his Example would ſeduce 'em to the Devil, could by his Precepts be conducing to their Salvation. This I ſay, they might doubt; and not without ſome reaſonable Grounds; and not without the Opinions of two of the Fathers, *viz.* St. *Cyprian*, and St. *Origen* to Authorize their Diſtruſt.

But to remove this Doubt, and to invalidate the Authorities of thoſe Fathers, the ſix and twentieth Article of Religion was thus Eſtabliſhed by the Convocations abovementioned.

Article 26.

Although in the viſible Church the Evil be ever mingled with the Good, and ſometime the Evil have chief Authority in the Miniſtration of the Word and Sacraments: Yet for as much as they do not the ſame in their own Name, but in Chriſt's, and do Miniſter by his Commiſſion and Authority, we may uſe their Miniſtery both in hearing the Word of God, and in receiving the Sacraments. Neither is the effect of Chriſt's Ordinance taken away by by their Wickedness, nor the Grace of God's Gifts diminished from such, as by Faith, and rightly do receive the Sacraments Ministred unto them; which are effectual, because of Christ's Institution and Promise, although they be Ministred by evil Men.

Nevertheless it appertaineth to the Discipline of the Church, that enquiry be made of evil Ministers: And that they be accused by those that have knowledge of their Offences; and finally being found Guilty by just Judgment be deposed.

Here is a most manifest Distinction made between the Man and the Priest. Between the regard to his Person, and the respect to his Function.

I will shew anon, that Mr. *Collier* himself has made this very Distinction, when he is pleased to approve of the Characters of *Joida* and *Mathan* in the *Athalia* of *Racine*.

If any Man has in any Play expos'd a Priest, as a Priest, and with an intimation, that as ſuch, his Character is ridiculous: I will agree heartily to condemn both the Play and the Author. I am confident no Man can defend ſuch an Impiety; and whoever is guilty of it, my Advice to him is, that he acknowlege his Error, that he repent of it and ſin no more.

I confeſs I do not remember any ſuch Character, Mr. *Collier*, who is more converſant with bad Plays than any Man that I know, perhaps may.

Mr. *Collier* in this Chapter produces many Inſtances of the Characters of Prieſts in the Poems of Heathen Writers; he is extreamly delighted with the Diſtinctions of their Habits, with the Show and Splendour in which they appear'd. The Crown and guilt Scepter of *Chryſes*, with the valuable Ranſom which he had in his Power, are Objects that gratifie his vain Imagination extreamly. He is indeed ſo rapt with his

ſplend-

ſplendid Ideas of *Chryſes*, *Laocoon*, and *Chloreus*, that to uſe his own Phraſe, he *runs riot* upon their Deſcription from *page* 112 to 118. he ſeems to have quite laid aſide the Thoughts of the *twelve poor Men who over-bore all the Oppoſitions of Power and Learning*, in pag. 81.

He now talks of nothing but great Families, great Places, wealthy and honourable Marriages, fine Cloaths, and in ſhort, of all the Pomps and Vanities of this wicked World. To give him his Due, as in ſome Places of his Book he criticizes more like a Pedant than a Scholar; argues more like a Sophiſter than a right Reaſoner, and rallies more like a Waterman than a Gentleman; ſo in this Place he talks more like a Herald-Painter than a Prieſt, and inſiſts more upon Pedigrees and Coats of Arms, than on moral Virtues or a generous Education.

He tells us the *Jewiſh* and *Egyptian* Prieſts, the *Perſian Magi*, and *Dru-*

 ids

ids of *Gaul* were all at the *upper end of the Government*, p. 131. What then? What is that to us, any more than if they were uſed to ſit at the upper end of the Table? No doubt this Gentleman's Affection for ſuch a Seat, furniſh'd him with this florid and metaporical Expreſſion.

In p. 132. He ſays *the Prieſthood was for ſome time confin'd to the Patrician Order.* Very well: we know the Reaſon of that; but with Submiſſion, that is not the ſame thing as if the *Patrician* Order had been confin'd to the Prieſthood. However, this Gentleman's Meaning is plain; certainly if he were Pope, he would renounce the Title of *Servus Servorum Dei.*

He quotes *Tully* for his Approba-
P. 133. tion of the ſame Perſon's being ſet at the Head both of Religion and Government. What does he mean by this? What Occaſion is there of this Quo-

Quotation, in our Country? Is not our King both at the Head of our Religion and Government? When Mr. *Collier* allows him one, perhaps he will not deny him the other.

But to come to his Meaning (if he has any) thro' all this vain Stuff. I take it, he would give us to understand, that in all Ages the Function of a Prieſt was held to be a very honourable Function. Did Mr. *Collier* ever meet with any Body Fool enough to engage him to aſſert that?

He tells us that Men of the firſt Quality; nay, Kings and Emperors have been employ'd in the ſacred Miniſtry: And I can tell him that Kings and Emperors have been in all Ages expos'd on the Stage; their Ambition, Tyrannies and Cruelties, all the Follies and Vices which were Conſequences of their arbitrary Power and ungovern'd Appetites, have been laid open to the Peoples View.

They have been puniſh'd, depos'd, and put to Death on the Stage; yet never any King complain'd of the Theater, or the Poets. On the contrary, all great Princes have cheriſh'd and ſupported them ſo long as they themſelves were great; till they have diminiſh'd in their own Characters, and turn'd to Bigotry and Enthuſiaſm; and of this a living Inſtance might be given.

Yet, 1. Kings have a Relation to the Deity.

They are his Deputies and Vicegerents on Earth.

2*ly*. They are poſſeſs'd of a very important Office. And,

3*ly*. Their Function has been in Poſſeſſion of Eſteem in all Ages and Countries.

That Men of Quality have always been, and are now employ'd in the ſacred Miniſtry, is evidently true; and I could heartily wiſh that more were

ſtill

ſtill employ'd in it: So ſhould the moſt honourable Office be executed by the moſt honourable Hands. So ſhould we behold Men of Birth, Title, and Heraldry, deſpiſing tinſel Shew, Pageantry, and all Mr. *Collier*'s beloved Bells, Bawbles, and Trinkets. And preferring Decency, Humility, Charity, and other Chriſtian Virtues, to ſhining Ornaments; or even the *upper End of a Government.* How ill ſuch temporal Pride agrees with the Perſon and Character of a truly pious and exemplary Divine, I will not pretend to determine. I will only tranſcribe the Words of a learn'd and honour'd Miniſter of the Church, to this purpoſe; and that is the reverend Mr. *Hales* of *Eaton.*

Vid. his Tract concerning Schiſm. p. 224, 225.

'For we have believ'd him that hath 'told us, *That in Jeſus Chriſt there is 'neither high nor low; and that in giving 'Honour, every Man ſhould be ready to 'prefer another before himſelf*; which

Say-

'Sayings cut off all Claim most certainly to Superiority, by Title of Christianity, except Men can think that these things were spoken only to poor and private Men. Nature and Religion agree in this, that neither of them hath a hand in this Heraldry of *secundum sub & supra*; all this comes from Composition and Agreement of Men among themselves. Wherefore this Abuse of Christianity, to make it *Lacquey* to Ambition, is a Vice for which I have no extraordinary Name of Ignominy, and an ordinary I will not give it, lest you should take so transcendent a Vice to be but trivial.

Here is not one Syllable of *Heraldry Regulated by* Garter, *and Blazon'd by* Stones. I would desire the Reader, immediately after this Paragraph from Mr. *Hales*, to consult Mr. *Collier* in *p.* 136. and to observe how he stickles for Place, and thrusts himself before the Gentlemen.

Coll. p. 135.

The

The Addition of Clerk is at least equal to that of Gentleman. How snappish and short his Clerkship is in his Periods; mark him, *were it otherwise, the Profession would in many Cases, be a kind of Punishment.* Good Heaven! To profess the Service of God would be a Punishment, if the Title of Clerk were not at least equal to that of Gentleman. Well, ---*The Heraldry is every Jot as safe in the Church, as 'twas in the State. When the Laity are taken leave of, not Gentleman but Clerk is usually Written.* And a little after. *The first Addition is not lost but covered.* Good Reader, return to Mr. *Hales*, that you may be reminded of the true Respect and Veneration that is due to his Memory; and to the rest of the Meek, the Modest, and the Humble Ministers of the Church: For while Mr. *Collier* is before you, you will be very apt to forget it.

I know many Reverend Clergymen now living, whoſe Names I cannot hear without Awe and Reverence: And why is that? Not from their Heraldry, but their Humility, their Humanity, their exceeding Learning, which is yet exceeded by their Modeſty; their exemplary Behaviour in their whole Lives and Converſations; their Charitable Cenſures, of Youthful Errors and Negligences, their fatherly and tender Admonitions, accompanyed with all ſweetneſs of Behaviour; and full of mild yet forcible Perſwaſion.

He were next to a *Manichean* that would not hold ſuch Men's Perſons in a degree of Veneration, next to their Profeſſion. But a Mr. *Prig*, a Mr. *Smirk*, and I'm afraid a Mr. *Collier* are Names implying Characters worthy of Averſion and Contempt.

Now let us take a View of Mr. *Collier*, as he appears upon the Stage; for

for while he is examining of Plays; I look upon him as one who has *Eloped* from his Pulpit and Strayed within the inclosures of the Theatre; and I do not see why the Players should not lay hold of him, and pound him till he has given them Absolution. Why does he abandon his Gown and Cassock to come Capering and Frisking, in his Lay-Doublet and Drawers, between the Scenes? Is he Master of the Revels? Is the Stage under his Discipline? *And is he fit to Correct the Theatre who is not fit to come into it?* v. Coll. p. 139.
He is not fit to come into it. First, Because his Office requires him in another place. And Secondly, Because he makes naughty uses of innocent Plays, and writes Baudy, and Blasphemous Comments, on the Poets Works.

Well, he has at length discovered a Play which is *an Exception to what he has observed in* France, (Coll. 124.)

124.) the Play is the *Athalia* of *Racine*. In this Play are the Characters of two Priests *Joida* and *Mathan*; of both which Mr. *Collier* is pleased to admit: By enquiring into his Reasons for Licensing this Play, we shall see in what manner he will allow a Priest to be represented on the Stage; and from thence we may guess how he himself would be contented to appear there also.

Joida (says he) *the High-Priest has a large Part, but then the Poet does him Justice in his Station; he makes him Honest and Brave, and gives him a shining Character throughout.* That's well. *Mathan is another Priest in the same Tragedy, he turns Renegado, and revolts from God to Baal.* That is not altogether so well. But has not the Poet done him Justice too, in giving him the Character that belong'd to him? Whether he has or not, Mr. *Collier* thinks he has made him ample reparation and

and more than amends, as you ſhall ſee. He goes on. *He is a very ill Man But* ---ay, now for the *BUT*. — He has turn'd Renegado, has revolted from God to *Baal*, is *poſitively* a very Ill-Man, But, what? O, *BUT makes a conſiderable Appearance.* There, now 'tis out, and all's well. If he has but *a gilt Crown, and Scepter, Scarlet and Embroidery in abundance*, let him rebel or revolt, he makes a good Figure, and it becomes him very well. Your Servant Mr. *Racine*, 'twas well for you that *Baal* gave good Benefices, and his Prieſts could afford to make a conſiderable Appearance: Or *Mathan*'s Revolt had not been ſo well taken at your Hands. But hold, Mr. *Collier* goes on.

I'm afraid the Reparation enlarges, and the Complement riſes. For the ſake of Connexion let us repeat.---

---*But makes a conſiderable Appearance.* And,---

Ay now, what can follow this *AND* in the Name of *Climax*? You

You ſhall ſee. ----*And is one of the Top of* Athalia's *Faction.*

Nay, then there is no more to be ſaid. If he had fine Cloaths, and was ſet at the Top, or rather at the *upper End* of a Faction too, he had his hearts Content: A reaſonable *Mathan* would have been ſatisfied with any one of thoſe Bleſſings. Tho' I would not anſwer for Mr. *Collier*'s Continence; at this time, eſpecially: he is ſo tranſported with Mr. *Racine*'s Bounty to *Mathan*, that he excuſes him frankly for ſhewing him a Renegado.

He goes on. ----*As for the Blemiſhes of his Life, they ſtick all upon his own Honour, and reach no farther than his Perſon.*

I think I have now kep't the Promiſe that I made not long ſince, to ſhew that Mr. *Collier* himſelf, when he is in the Humour, will allow of the Diſtinction betwixt the *Man* and the *Prieſt*, the Perſon and the Function.

But

But to ſhew that I can be as croſs as he; now when he would admit of this diſtinction, I ſhould rather ſay when he alledges it, it ſhall not by any means be granted him. Here is a renegade Prieſt, that revolts from the true God to *Baal*: And this Man is only branded with a Blemiſh on his Perſon. What, is it no Affront to his Function then? I take it to be no excuſe for him that he ſhould afterwards become a Prieſt of *Baal*. Sure Mr. *Collier* does not mean to make uſe of Mr. *Dryden*'s Key as he calls it, and ſay that *Prieſts of all Religions*, &c. Well, 'tis only a Blemiſh upon his Perſon; or if Mr. *Collier* pleaſes, becauſe he delights in Phraſes of Heraldry, 'tis only a Blot in his Scutcheon. Let Mr. *Collier* anſwer for this, to thoſe who have Authority to examine him further. He is in every Line growing more and more gracious to Mr. *Racine*. And now he is come to the very *top* or *upper-end* of his Civility; and ſays with a *bon grace* and *belle air*, that

——*in fine, the Play is a very religious Poem.*

Indeed! why then *in fine* we are tack'd about; then a Play *in fine*, may be a religious Poem it ſeems: Why then Sir *Martin* with his, *in fine*, here has quite unravel'd his own Plot. Ay, ay, the Play is a very religious Poem; if Faction and fine Cloaths wont make a religious Poem, it muſt be made of ſtrange Stuff indeed.

——*'Tis upon the Matter all Sermon and Anthem*——

O Lord! nay, now I proteſt Mr. *Collier* this muſt not be; nay now you're ſo infinitely obliging! fye, this is too much on t'other ſide: You quite forget the Fathers indeed Sir, and the Biſhop of *Arras*.

——*And if it were not deſign'd for the Theatre*—

Out

Out with it Man.——*I have nothing to Object.*

Why that's well, now he's come to himſelf. O' my Word, I was half afraid he would have play'd the *Mathan*, and have revolted to the Theatre. The Miſchief is, this naughty Theatre will be interloping; when Sermon and Anthem, become the Stage as ill, as Faction and fine Cloaths do the Pulpit: But Men ſometimes travel into Foreign Provinces for Variety.

I cannot forbear enquiring into one Example more, which this Gentleman offers us in the very next Page. *In the Hiſtory of Sir* John Oldcaſtle, *Sir* John, *Parſon of* Wrotham, *Swears, Games, Wenches, Pads, Tilts and Drinks; this is extremely bad.*

Extremely bad? Can any thing be worſe? and yet (ſays he) *Shakeſpear's* Sir John, *has ſome advantage in his Character.* Now who can forbear enquiring what advantage a Character can possibly have, consistent with such abominable Vices? First, *He appears loyal and Stout; he brings in Sir* John, Acton, *and other Rebels, Prisoners.* So! as 'tis in the *Spanish Fryar*, a Manifest Member of the Church Militant! That he was Stout, was plain before, from his Padding and Tilting. But this will not do; the advantage does not yet appear. No! why then.

--*He is rewarded by the King, and the Judge uses him civilly and with Respect.*

This Advantage appears still but coldly. Kings reward Spys and Executioners, and necessary Instruments of Policy and Punishment. And Judges are generally Men of Years, Temper and Wisdom, and use all Gentlemen with Civility. Ay, say you so? why then—*in short*— ay, now for the Iliads in a Nut-shell. Here is the *But* coming again, I had a glimpse of him just now. *ex. gr.*

In short he is represented Lewd, but *not* Little.

There is an Advantage for you now; *in short, Lewd* but not *Little.*

Concise and pretty! the Gentleman had best take it for a Motto, and have it annex'd to his Coat-Armour, when he can get *his Heraldry regulated by Garter, and blazon'd by Stones.*

Well, I confess I have been in an Error; I thought a Man never appear'd so very little, as when he appear'd extremely lewd. If I have undervalued Lewdness, I ask Mr. *Collier's* Pardon.

And the Disgrace falls rather on the Person than the Office.

Here again you see, he will allow this Distinction to all his Favourites. Here is the Person and the Function separated again; the Priest and the Man: In short, he answers himself so often, that I will dispute this Point no more with him.

But you may ſee what this poor Gentleman in the wretched Pride of his little Heart, thinks a ſufficient Alloy to make current a moſt diſſolute or impious Character. Though you expoſe a Prieſt revolting from God to *Baal*, yet if you let him make a conſiderable Figure, and place him at the Head of a Faction, all is well enough; and the Poem may be a *religious Poem*, &c. Shew another in Comedy, let him Swear, Game, Wench, Pad, Tilt and Drink, but withal let him keep good Company; let a Judge, or ſome Great Man treat him with Reſpect, that he may not appear little, though he appear lewd, and you give *ſome advantage to his Character*; at leaſt you will ſhew that he *underſtands his Poſt, and con-*
Ibid. *verſes with the Freedom of a Gentleman.*

In Page 122, Our Author has obſerv'd *how the Heathen Poets behav'd themſelves in the Argument. Prieſts ſel-*

dom

dom appear in their Plays ; and when they come, 'tis buſineſs of Credit that brings them. They are treated like Perſons of Condition ; they act up to their Relation, neither ſneak, nor prevaricate, nor do any thing unbecoming their Office.

Indeed when Men neither ſneak, nor prevaricate, nor do any thing unbecoming their Office in the World, they ought not to be repreſented otherwiſe on the Stage: Nay, they ought not to be expos'd at all in Comedy ; for the Characters expos'd there, ſhould be of thoſe only, who misbehave themſelves.

Let us ſuppoſe that the Character of this Author were to be ſhewn upon the Stage: he who ſhould repreſent him behaving himſelf as he ought, would be to blame, and that for theſe Reaſons.

Firſt, To repreſent him behaving himſelf as he ought, would be to repreſent him in the diſcharge of ſome part of his Holy Office, which is by no means fit to be ſhewn on the Stage; eſpecially in Comedy, where Mens Vices and Follies are expos'd: That would be to bring Mr. *Collier*'s Function, not his Perſon on the Stage, which is not to be permitted.

Secondly, He that ſhould repreſent Mr. *Collier* behaving himſelf as he ought, would very much miſrepreſent Mr. *Collier*, in reſpect to the Manners of his Character.

Let us take a ſlight Sketch of him as he preſents himſelf to us in his Book. Let Mr. *Collier* be repreſented as he is, not as he ought to be; that by ſeeing what he is, Mr. *Collier* may be aſham'd of what he is, and endeavour at what he ought to be.

And that the Inſtruction of the Repreſentation may not be loſt, let us borrow that Diſtinction which ſevers the Prieſt from the Man: If *Mathan*, and Sir *John* of *Wrotham*, have

done

done with it, they may lend it to us; 'tis for the uſe of an Humble Servant of theirs, and whenever the Humour takes 'em to Revolt, Pad, Tilt, Wench, Drink, and ſoforth, let 'em give us a Quarter of an Hours Notice, and they ſhall have it again.

Well, Our Author being thus divided, we will deſire the better Part of him, to take his Place in the Pit, and let the other appear to him like his evil Genius on the Stage.

Suppoſe the Gentleman in the Scene to appear very intent upon the very Obſcene Comedies of *Ariſtophanes*, *quær*. Whether the Perſon in the Pit, beholding how very ill this becomes him, will not think that he might with much more Decency, betake himſelf to his *Septuagint*? *Coll.* p.40.44.

Mr. *Collier* on the Stage ſhall anathematiſe the Poets, and tell 'em in plain Terms, they ſhould be excommunicated, and that *they are not fit to*

come

Coll. 139. *come into the Church. Quær.* whether Mr. *Collier*, in the Pit, will not think it had been more becoming his Character, to have invited and exhorted them to it?

Mr. *Collier* on the Stage ſhall behave himſelf with all the Arrogance, p. 136. and little Pride of a ſpruce *Pedant*, that the Gentlemen in the Pit may be induc'd to practiſe the Meekneſs and Humility of a Chriſtian Divine. The former, ſhall pervert V. *moſt part of Mr.* Collier's *Quotations.* and miſconſtrue every thing that is ſaid to him, that the latter may learn to uſe Juſtice, Candor, and Sincerity, in his Interpretations.

The Player *Collier* ſhall call the Gentlemen that he converſes with, V. *Pref.* 81. 63, 175. Foot-pads, Buffoons, Slaves, *&c.* that the Spectator *Collier* may remember they are Chriſtians, and ſhould be catechis'd by other Names.

Mr. *Collier*, on the Stage, ſhall rack Bawdery and Obſcenity out of modeſt

modeſt and innocent Expreſſions; and having extorted it, he ſhall ſcourge it, not out of Chaſtiſement but Wantonneſs; he ſhall forget, that *ſometimes to report a Fault is to repeat* P. 71.
it. The Spectator in the Pit ſhall plainly perceive, that he loves to look on naked Obſcenity; and that he only flogs it, as a ſinful Pædagogue *Coll.*
ſometimes laſhes a pretty Boy, that Ch. 1, 2.
looks lovely in his Eyes, for Reaſons beſt known to himſelf.

Caſtigo te non quod odio habeam, ſed quod amem.

Mr. *Collier*, on the Stage, ſhall ridicule, rail at, and condemn all Plays whatſoever: He ſhall tire himſelf, and his Audience, with his Inveteracy and Exclamations againſt them. Which done, he ſhall all on the ſudden, and, that there may be ſomething ſurprizing, and *præter expectatum* in his Character, from a Perſecutor, become a Promoter of the

Drama:

Drama: He ſhall be as furious a *Critick* as he was a *Bigot*; and give the beſt Rules and Inſtructions of which he is capable, for the Compoſure of Comedy. He ſhall talk in all the Pedantical Cant of Fable, Intrigue, Diſcovery, of Unities of Time, Place, and Action. But leſt this Behaviour in Mr. *Collier's* Character ſhould appear inconſiſtent, and a violation of the Precept of *Horace*.

V. *from* P. 209. *to* 228, *and forwards.*

——*Servetur ad imum,*
Qualis ab incepto proceſſerit; & ſibi conſtet.

His Vanity ſhall bear proportion with his Diſſimulation; his Ignorance ſhall be as great as his Malice; and he ſhall not be able to deviate from his inveterate Zeal againſt Plays; for he ſhall not appear to underſtand one Syllable of the Rules of Writing, but ſhall miſlead Poetry as much by his Inſtructions, as he has perverted it by his Interpretations; he ſhall favour his Adverſaries without

out

out obliging them; the Zeal of his Character ſhall be preſerv'd even in his own deſpite; and his Devotion, in this Particular, ſhall be the Child of his Ignorance: For he can make but

---- *Lame Miſchief tho' he mean it well.* P. 104.

And if Plays are pernicious, Mr. *Collier* ſhall only be wicked in his Wiſhes, he ſhall be acquitted in his Performances; his Inſtigations to Poetry ſhall prove checks upon it. He ſhall appear mounted upon a falſe *Pegaſus*, like a *Lancaſhire* Witch upon an imaginary Horſe, the Fantom ſhall be unbridled, and the Broom- P. 230.
ſtick made viſible.

At this *Cataſtrophe*, Mr. *Collier*, in the Pit, ſhall exclaim like *Flecknoe*, and with very little variation.

O why did'ſt thou on Learning fix a Brand,
And rail at Arts thou did'ſt not underſtand?

Now, leſt the Poet who ſhall undertake this Character, ſhould be gra-

gravell'd in the imitation of the Stile of this elaborate Writer, let him take these few Instances of his allusive and highly metaphorical Expressions, for Patterns; *viz. running riot upon Smut: A Poem with a Litter of Epithets, like a Bitch overstock'd with Puppies: Sucking the Sense to skin and bone: A Fancy slip-stocking high: The upper-end of a Government: A whole Kennel of Beaux after a Woman, &c.* For his Elegancy, these are Originals: *Learning a Spaniel to set: This belike is the meaning: Three of the biggest of Four: Big Alliances, Men*
See p. 12. *of the biggest Consideration for sense, &c.*
27, 34, *To marry up a Top-Lady*: Cum multis
92, 131, aliis.
132,
225, 'Tis a strange thing that a Man
233, &c. should write such Stuff as this, who is capable of making the following
Coll. Observation.
205.

Offensive Language, like Offensive Smells, does but make a Man's Senses a burthen, and affords him nothing but loathing and Aversion.

For

For these Reasons, 'tis a Maxim in good Breeding never to shock the Senses or Imagination. Ibid.

Indeed there are few things which distinguish the manner of a Man's Breeding and Conversation, more visibly, than the Metaphors which he uses in Writing; I mean in writing from himself, and in his own Name and Character, A Metaphor is a similitude in a Word, a short Comparison; and it is used as a similitude, to illustrate and explain the meaning. The Variety of *Ideas* in the Mind, furnish it with variety of Matter for Similitudes; and those *Ideas* are only so many Impressions made on the Memory, by the force and frequency of external Objects.

Pitiful and mean Comparisons, proceed from pitiful and mean *Ideas*; and such *Ideas* have their beginning from a familiarity with such Objects. From this Author's poor and filthy Metaphors

Metaphors and Similitudes, we may learn the Filthineſs of his Imagination; and from the Uncleanneſs of that, we may make a reaſonable gueſs at his rate of Education, and thoſe Objects with which he has been moſt converſant and familiar.

To conclude with him in this Chapter; I will only ſay that no Man living has a greater reſpect for a good Clergy-man, nor more contempt for an ill one, than my ſelf; the former I have often been proud to ſhew, the latter never fell in my way till now. I never yet introduced the Character of a Clergy-man in any of my Plays, excepting that little Apparition of *Say-grace*, in the *Double-Dealer*; and I am very indifferent whether ever the Gown appear upon the Stage, or not: If it does, I think it ſhould not be worn by the Character of a good Man; for ſuch a one ought not to be made the Compa-

nion

nion of foolish Characters. If ever it is shewn there, it ought to be hung loosely on the shoulders of such a one as I have lately instanced; but to no other end, than to demonstrate that even the sacred Habit is abus'd by some; but by their Characters and Manners the Audience may observe what manner of Men they are. And no question but if our Author, in the Pit, did behold his Counterpart on the Stage, thus egregiously to play the Fool in his *Pontificalibus*, *the rebuke would strike stronger upon his sense*, and prove more effectual to his Reformation. Coll. 111.

I come now to his Chapter of the Immorality of the Stage.

His Objections here are rather Objections against Comedy in general, than against mine, or any bodies Comedies in particular. He says the Sparks that *marry up the Top-Ladies*, and are rewarded with Wives and P. 142.

Fortunes in the laſt *Acts*, are generally debauch'd Characters. In anſwer to this, I refer to my firſt and ſecond Propoſition. He is a little particular in his Remarks upon *Valentine*, in *Love for Love*. He ſays,

Ibid. *This Spark, the Poet would paſs for a Perſon of Vertue; but he ſpeaks too late.*

I know who, and what he is, that always ſpeaks too ſoon. Why is he to be paſs'd for a Perſon of Vertue? Or where is it ſaid that his Character makes extraordinary Pretenſions to it! *Valentine* is in *Debt*, and in *Love*; he has honeſty enough to cloſe with a hard Bargain, rather than not pay his Debts, in the firſt *Act*; and he has Generoſity and Sincerity enough, in the laſt *Act*, to ſacrifice every thing to his Love; and when he is in danger of loſing his Miſtreſs, thinks every thing elſe of little worth. This, I hope, may be allow'd a Reaſon for the Lady to ſay, *He has Vertues*: They are

are ſuch in reſpect to her; and her once ſaying ſo, in the laſt *Act*, is all the notice that is taken of his *Vertue* quite thro' the Play.

Mr. *Collier* ſays, he *is Prodigal*. He was prodigal, and is ſhewn, in the firſt *Act* under hard Circumſtances, which are the Effects of his Prodigality. That he is unnatural and undutiful, I don't underſtand: He has indeed a very unnatural Father; and if he does not very paſſively ſubmit to his Tyranny and barbarous Uſage, I conceive there is a Moral to be apply'd from thence to ſuch Fathers. That he is *profane* and *obſcene*, is a falſe Accuſation, and without any Evidence. In ſhort, the Character is a mix'd Character; his Faults are fewer than his good Qualities; and, as the World goes, he may paſs well enough for the beſt Character in a Comedy; where even the beſt muſt be ſhewn to have Faults, that the best Spectators may be warn'd not to think too well of themselves.

P. 171. 172. He quotes the *Old Batchelor* twice in this Chapter. His first Quotation is made with his usual assurance and fair dealing.

If any one would understand what the Curse of all tender-hearted Women is, Bellmour *will inform him. What is it then? 'Tis the Pox.*

Here he makes a Flourish upon ill Nature's being recommended as a Guard of Vertue and of Health, *&c.*

The whole Matter of Fact is no more than this.

Lucy to *Belmour, Act 5. Scene 2.*

If you do deceive me, the Curse of all kind tender-hearted Women light upon you.

Bell. *That's as much as to say, The Pox take me.*

It is his Interpretation; and it is agreeable to his Character. He is a Debauchee, and he thinks there is but one way for Women to be kind and

and tender-hearted; and, I think, his threat'ning them with ſuch a Curſe as the conſequence of too much eaſineſs, does not ſeem to recommend the Vice at all, but rather to forbid it: His very Leudneſs, in this place, is made moral and inſtructive.

I am very glad our Author is in ſuch Circumſtances, in this Chapter, that he can bear the ſight of that *Helliſh Syllable, Pox*; and prevail with himſelf to write it at its full length. *Non ita pridem.* In Page 82. he loves his Love with a P---but no naming: That is not like a Cavalier. What *Ermin* was ever an Inſtance of superfine Nicety comparable to Mr. *Collier*? I will not ſay, what *Cat*? Tho' if I ſhould, I can quote a *Spaniſh* Proverb to juſtifie the Compariſon.

El gato ſcaldado tiene miedo de agua fria.

He makes one Quotation more, to what purpoſe indeed I know not; but I will repeat it, in Juſtice to him,

 becauſe

becauſe it is the laſt that he has made, and the firſt fair one. *Old Batch.* Act 4. *Belinda* to *Sharp.*

P, 172. ----*Where did you get this excellent Talent of Railing?*

Sharp.---*Madam, the Talent was born with me.* ---- *I confeſs I have taken care to improve it, to qualifie me for the Society of Ladies.*

Theſe are the Words juſt as the Gentleman quotes 'em; but why, or wherefore, he is not pleas'd to diſcover; for he ſays not one Syllable, for, nor againſt 'em: I ſuppoſe he thinks the Proof plain, and the Evidence firm without a Coroborator.

I hope the Reader will not forget, that theſe Inſtances are produc'd, to prove that I have encourag'd Immorality in my Plays. I thought the Expreſſion, above-mentioned, had been a gentle Reproof to the Ladies that are addicted to railing; and ſince Mr. *Collier* has not ſaid that it *muſt*

mean

mean the contrary, I don't ſee why it may not be underſtood ſo ſtill ?

I have now gone thorough with all Mr. *Collier's* Quotations; I have been as ſhort as I could poſſibly in their Vindication; I have avoided all Recriminations, and have not ſo much as made one Citation from any of my Plays in favour of them: Whatever they contain of Morality, or Inveſtives againſt Folly and Vice, is no more than what ought to be in them; therefore I do not urge it as a Merit.

My Buſineſs was not to paint, but to waſh; not to ſhew Beauties, but to wipe off Stains.

Mr. *Collier* has indeed given me an opportunity of reforming many Errors, by obliging me to a review of my own Plays.

Dum relego ſcripſiſſe pudet, quia plurima
Cerno
Me quoq; qui feci, Judice, digna lini.

But I muſt affirm, that they are only Errors occaſion'd by Inadvertency or Inexperience, and that I am conſcious of nothing that can make me liable to his Cenſure, or rather Slander. I am as ready to own the Advantages I have received from his Book, as to demonſtrate the Wrongs; if I reſent the latter, it is becauſe they were intended me; and if I do not thank him for the other, it is becauſe they were not: He would have poiſon'd me, but he overdoſed it, and the Exceſs of his Malice has been my Security.

To give him his due, he ſeems every where to write more from Prejudice, than Opinion; he rails when he ſhould reaſon; and for gentle Reproofs, uſes ſcurrilous Reproaches. He looks upon his Adverſaries to be his Enemies; and to juſtifie his Opinion in that Particular, before he has done with them,

he

he makes them ſo. If there is any Spirit in his Arguments, it evaporates and flies off unſeen, thro' the heat of his Paſſion. His Paſſion does not only make him appear in many Places to be in the wrong, but it alſo makes him appear to be conſcious of it. That which ſhews the Face of Wit in his Writing, has indeed no more than the Face; for the Head is wanting. Wit is at the beſt but the *Sign* to good underſtanding; it is hung out to recommend the Entertainment which may be found within; And it is very well when the Invitation can be made good. As the outward Form of Godlineſs is Hypocriſie, which very often conceals Irreligion and Immorality; ſo is Wit alſo very often an Hypocriſie, a Superficies glaz'd upon falſe Judgment, a good Face ſet on a bad Underſtanding.

It is a Mask which Mr. *Collier* ſometimes wears, but it does not fit the

the Mold of his Face; he presumes too much on the Security of his Disguise, and very often ventures till he is discover'd: He does not know himself in his Foreign Dress, and from thence concludes that no body else can. His Ancestor of honour'd Memory, recorded in *Æsop*, miscarried thro' the same Self-sufficiency. Mr. *Collier*, when he cloathed himself in the Lion's Skin, should have thought of an Expedient to have conceal'd his Ears: But, it may be, he is proud of them, and thinks it proper to shew that he has them *both*, and at their full length.

He has put himself to some pain to shew his Reading; and his Reading is such, that it puts us to pain to behold it. He discovers an ill Taste in Books, and a worse Digestion. He has swallow'd so much of the Scum of Authors, that the overflowing of his own Gall was superfluous to make

it

it riſe upon his Stomach. But he ought in good Manners to have ſtept aſide, and not to have been thus nau-ſeous and offenſive to the Noſes of the whole Country. But as his Reading would not ſtay with him, ſo his Wri-ting ran away with him.

Ben Johnſon, in his Diſcoveries, ſays, *There be ſome Men are born only to ſuck the Poiſon of Books.* Habent venenum pro victu imo pro deliciis. *And ſuch are they that only reliſh the obſcene and foul things in Poets; which makes the Profeſ-ſion tax'd: But by whom? Men that watch for it*, &c. Something farther in the ſame Diſcoveries, He is ſpeaking again very much to our purpoſe; for it is in juſtification of preſenting vici-ous and fooliſh Characters on the Stage in Comedy. It ſeems ſome People were angry at it then; let us compare his Picture of them, with the Characters of thoſe who quarrel at it now. *It ſufficeth* (ſays he) *I* *know*

Johnſ. Diſc. P. 702.

Johnſ. Diſc. P. 714.

know what kind of Persons I displease, Men bred in the declining and decay of Vertue, betrothed to their own Vices; that have abandoned, or prostituted their good Names; hungry and ambitious of Infamy, invested in all Deformity, enthrall'd to Ignorance and Malice, of a hidden and conceal'd Malignity, and that hold a concomitancy with all Evil.

'Tis strange that Mr. *Collier* should oversee these two Passages, when he was simpling in the same Field where they both grow. This is pretty plain; because in the 51st Page of his Book he presents you with a Quotation from the same *Discoveries*, as one intire Paragraph, tho' severally collected from the 706 and 717th Pages of the Original; so that he has read both before, and beyond these Passages. But a Man that looks in a Glass often, walks away, and forgets his resemblance.

Mr. *Collier's* Vanity in pretending

to

to Criticiſm, has extremely betray'd his Ignorance in the Art of Poetry; this is manifeſt to all that underſtand it. And methinks his Affectation of ſeeming to have read every thing, ſometimes betrays him to Confeſſions that are not much to his Advantage. I wonder he is not aſham'd to own, that he is ſo well acquainted with the ἐκκλησιαζύσαι of *Ariſtophanes*. The Dialogues of *Aretine*, or *Aloïſia*, are not more obſcene than that Piece. The Author there, as Mr. *Bays* ſays, *does egad name the thing directly*, and that in above a hundred Places. But perhaps Mr. *Collier* meant to veil that Play under a *Miſnommer* (to uſe his own Phraſe); and when he call'd it *Concianotores*, thought we could not diſcover, that in ſpite of his Artifice, or his Ignorance, he *muſt* mean no other than the leud *Concionatrices*, or Parliament-Women of *Ariſtophanes*. He has indeed rak'd together a

Coll. P. 44.

ſtrange

ſtrange number of Authors Names: But as *Gideon's* Army of Two and thirty thouſand was order'd to be reduc'd to Three hundred; ſo his rabble of Citations, without any loſs to him, might be reduc'd to a much leſs number: But his Buſineſs is not *Diſcipline*, but *Tumult*. He appears like Captain *Tom* at the Head of a People that are ſhuffled together, neither the World, nor they, nor *He*, can tell why; but ſince they are met, Plunder is the Word, and the Play-houſe is firſt to be demoliſh'd.

He has outdone *Bays* in his grand Dance; nay, the Heathen Philoſophers in their Notions of the grand Chaos, never imagin'd a greater confuſion. All Religions, all Countries, all Ages, are jumbled together, to explode what all Religions, all Countries, and all Ages have allow'd. He is not contented with his *Battalia*, compounded of *Bramins*, *Brachmans*, *Muf-*

ties

ties, Councils, Fathers, the Bishop of *Arras*, &c. But the Philosophers, nay, the very Poets themselves are press'd to the Service.

Cicero endeavour'd with all his might to get himself a Name in Poetry; and *Aristotle* preferr'd *Tragedy* even to *Philosophy*. But Mr. *Collier* has converted them both; in short, between him, and the Bishop of *Arras*, they have been seduc'd and inviegl'd over to the other side.

He pretends to triumph in the heart of *Parnassus*, and has sown dissention in the bosoms of some of the chief Proprietors. *Ovid* and the *Plain Dealer* are revolted, and take Arms against their Brethren, while Mr. *Collier* sings with *Lucan* and *Hudibras* of--*Civil Fury*, &c.

——————*populumq; potentem.*
In sua victrici Conversum viscera dextra:
Cognatasq; acies----

Bays against *Bays*--& *Pila minantia pilis.*

I wish his Seeds of Sedition were not

not ſcatter'd elſewhere ; for here I
think they will hardly thrive. What
effect his Doctrine in private Families
P. 139. will have, I know not, when the Superiority comes to be diſputed between the Country-Gentlemen, and
their Chaplains; or rather, as Mr. *Collier* has eſtabliſh'd it, between the
Chaplains, and their Country-Gentle-
man.

I am not the only one who look on this Pamphlet of his to be a Gun levell'd at the whole Laity, while the ſhot only glances on the Theatre; what he means by the Attack, or what may be its Conſequences, I know not; and I ſuppoſe he cares not: *Bellum inchoant inertes, fortes finiunt.* But there are thoſe who will not be diſpleas'd at an occaſion of making Recriminations. With reſpect to his Parts, it is no wiſe thing to give any body an Example of ſearching into Books for negligent and fooliſh Expreſſions. Divines have ſometimes forgot themſelves in Controverſial Writings; Diſputes begun, or pretended to have been begun on Points of Faith, have ended in ſcurrilous and perſonal Reflections;and from Tracts of Divinity, have degenerated into *Paſquils* and *Lampoons.* That Mr. *Collier* has laid the Foundation of ſuch a Controverſie, I think is apparent; but I hope his Credit is not ſufficient to engage any body to go on with the Building.

He has aſſaulted the Town in the Seat of their principal, and moſt reaſonable Pleaſure. Down with the Theatre right or wrong. *Delenda eſt Carthago,*let the Conſequence be what it will. That was a very raſh Maxim; and if *Cato* had liv'd to have ſeen its Effects, he would have repented it. To perſecute an Allie (and that deſires no more than to continue in our Alliance) as an Enemy, is a

I weak,

weak, and barbarous Piece of Policy.

Perſecution makes Men perſevere in the right; and Perſecution may make 'em perſiſt in the wrong. Men may, by ill uſage, be irritated ſometimes to aſſert and maintain, even their very Errors. Perhaps there is a vicious Pride of triumphing in the worſt of the Argument, which is very prevailing with the Vanity of Mankind; I cannot help thinking that our Author is not without his ſhare of this Vanity. I think truly he had a fair appearance of Right on his ſide in the Title Page of his Book; but with reaſon I think I may alſo affirm, that by his miſ-management he has very much weak'ned his Title. He that goes to Law for more than his Right, makes his Pretenſions, even to that which is his Right, ſuſpected; as a true Story loſes its Credit, when related from the Mouth of a known Liar.

Mr. *Collier's* many falſe Citations, make

make his true ſuſpected; and his miſapplication of his true Citations, very much arraign both his Judgment and Sincerity. His Authorities from the Fathers (with all due reſpect to them) are certainly no more to the purpoſe, than if he had cited the two *Attick* Laws againſt the Licentiouſneſs of the Old Comedy; in Truth not ſo much: For the Invectives of the Fathers, were levell'd at the Cruelty of the *Gladiators*, and the Obſcenity of the *Partomimes*. If ſome of them have confounded the *Drama* with ſuch ſpectacles, it was an overſight of Zeal very allowable in thoſe days; and in the Infaney of Chriſtianity, when the Religion of the Heathens was intermingled with their Poetry and Theatral Repreſentations; thereforc Chriſtians, then, might very well be forbidden to frequent even the beſt of them. As for our Theatres, St. *Auſtin* and *Lactantius* knew no more of them,

 than

Vid. St. *Aust. de Civ. Dei. l. 16. c. 9. & Lact. de fals. Sap.* 23.

than they did of the *Antipodes*; and they might with as much difficulty have been perswaded, that the former would in after-times be tolerated in a Christian State, as that the latter wou'd be receiv'd for a manifest and common Truth, and made intelligible to the Capacity of every Child.

To what end has he made such a Bugbear of the Theatre? Why would he possess the Minds of weak and melancholick People with such frightful *Ideas* of a poor Play? Unless to sowre the humours of the People of most leisure, that they might be more apt to mis-employ their vacant hours. It may be there is not any where a People, who should less be debarr'd of innocent Diversions, than the People of *England*. I will not argue this Point; but I will strengthen my Observation with one Parallel to it from *Polybius*; That excellent Author, who always moralizes in his History, and instructs

as

as faithfully as he relates; in his 4th Book, attributes the the Ruin of *Cynethia* by the *Ætolians*, in plain Terms, to their degeneracy from their *Arcadian* Anceſtors, in their neglect of Theatral and Muſical Performances. The *Cynethians* (ſays my Author) had their Situation the fartheſt *North* in all *Arcadia*; they were ſubjected to an inclement and uncertain Air, and for the moſt part cold and melancholick; and, for this reaſon, they of all People ſhould laſt have parted with the innocent and wholeſome Remedies, which the Diverſions of Muſick adminiſtred to that ſowrneſs of Temper, and ſullenneſs of Diſpoſition, which of neceſſity they muſt partake from the Diſpoſition and Influence of their Climate; " For they no ſooner fell to " neglect theſe wholeſome Inſtitu- " tion, when they fell into Diſſen- " tions and Civil Diſcords, and grew " at length into ſuch depravity of " Man-

Vid. *Tranſl. by Sir* H. Sheer, *Vol.* 2. *p.* 46.

" Manners, that their Crimes in num-
" ber and meaſure ſurpaſs'd all Na-
" tions of the *Greeks* beſide.

He gives us to underſtand, that their *Chorus's* on the Theatres, their frequent Aſſemblies of young People, Men and Women, mingling in Muſical Performances, were not inſtituted by their Anceſtors out of Wantonneſs and Luxury, but out of Wiſdom; from a deliberated and effectual Policy, and for the Reaſons above noted. Much more might be cited from *Polybius*, who has made a very conſiderable digreſſion on this occaſion.

The Application of what I have borrow'd, is very plain. Is there in the World a Climate more uncertain than our own? And which is a natural Conſequence, Is there any where a People more unſteady, more apt to diſcontent, more *ſaturnine*, *dark*, and *melancholick* than our ſelves? Are we not of all People the most unfit to be alone, and most unsafe to be trusted with our selves? Are there not more Self-murderers, and melancholick Lunaticks in *England*, heard of in one Year, than in a great part of *Europe* besides? From whence are all our Sects, Schisms, and innumerable Subdivisions in Religion? Whence our Plots, Conspiracies, and Seditions? Who are the the Authors and Contrivers of these things? Not they who frequent the Theatres and Consorts of Musick. No, if they had, it may be Mr. *Collier's* Invective had not been levell'd that way; his *Gun-Powder-Treason* Plot upon Musick and Plays (for he says *Musick is as dangerous as* p. 279. *Gun-Powder)* had broke out in another Place, and all his False-Witnesses been summoned elsewhere.

FINIS.

Appendix

Three leaves from the Ashley copy: half title, title page, and D6.

AMENDMENTS
OF
Mr. COLLIER's
False and Imperfect CITATIONS, &c.

ADVERTISEMENT.

AN Overſight in reading *Superſtition* for ſuppoſition in Mr. *Collier*'s Book, *p.* 64. occaſion'd a Miſtake in a ſmall Number of theſe Amendments, which were firſt Printed off; but in the remainder of the Impreſſion, the Remark grounded on that Miſtake is omitted, Care being taken to have that Leaf re-printed.

AMENDMENTS

OF

Mr. COLLIER's

False and Imperfect CITATIONS, &c.

From the { OLD BATCHELOUR, DOUBLE DEALER, LOVE for LOVE, MOURNING BRIDE.

By the Author of those Plays.

Quem recitas meus est ô Fidentine Libellus,
Sed male dum recitas incipit esse tuus.

Mart.

Graviter, & iniquo animo, maledicta tua paterer, si te scirem Judicio magis, quam morbo animi, petulantia ista uti. Sed, quoniam in te neque modum, neque modestiam ullam animadverto, respondebo tibi: uti, si quam maledicendo voluptatem cepisti, eam male-audiendo amittas.

Salust. Decl.

LONDON,
Printed for *J. Tonson* at the *Judge's Head* in *Fleet street*, near the *Inner-Temple-Gate*, 1698.

ERRATA.

Page 7. line 23. for *worst* read *worse*; p. 105. l. 13. read *Pantomimes*, p. 107. l. 3. r. *Cynetha*.

good Advice, and requir'd an Anſwer, but the Direction for the Superſcription was forgot. If the good Gentlewoman is yet in being, I deſire her to receive my Thanks for her good Counſel, and for her Approbation of all the Comedy, that Word alone excepted.

That Lady *Plyant* talks ***Smut*** in the ſame Sentence, lies yet upon Mr. *Collier* to prove. His bare Aſſertion without an Inſtance, is not ſufficient. If he can prove that there is downright *Smut* in it, why e'en let him take it for his pains: I am willing to part with it.

His next Objection is, that Sir *Paul*, who he obſerves bears the Character of a Fool, makes mention too often of the word *Providence*; for ſays Mr. *Collier*, *the meaning muſt be* (by the way; that *muſt* is a little hard upon me) *that Pro-* p. 62.

vidence

vidence is a ridiculous Suppoſition; and that none but Blockheads pretend to Religion. What will it avail me in this place to ſignifie my own meaning, when this modeſt Gentleman ſays, I *muſt mean* quite contrary?

Lady Froth is pleaſed to call Jehu *a Hackney Coachman.* (Ibid.)

Lady *Froth's* words are as follow— *Our Jehu was a Hackney Coachman when my Lord took him.* Which is as much as to ſay, that the Coachman's Name is *Jehu*: And why might it not be *Jehu* as well as *Jeremy*, or *Abraham*, or *Joſeph*, or any other Jewiſh or Chriſtian Name? *Brisk* deſires that this may be put into a Marginal Note in Lady Froth's Poem.

This Mr. *Collier* ſays, is meant to *burleſque the Text, and Comment under one.* What Text, or what Comment,

or